SPORTS SUPERSTARS

CHLOE KIM

BY GOLRIZ GOLKAR

TORQUE

BELLWETHER MEDIA • MINNEAPOLIS, MN

Torque brims with excitement perfect for thrill-seekers of all kinds. Discover daring survival skills, explore uncharted worlds, and marvel at mighty engines and extreme sports. In *Torque* books, anything can happen. Are you ready?

This edition first published in 2024 by Bellwether Media, Inc.

No part of this publication may be reproduced in whole or in part without written permission of the publisher. For information regarding permission, write to Bellwether Media, Inc., Attention: Permissions Department, 6012 Blue Circle Drive, Minnetonka, MN 55343.

Library of Congress Cataloging-in-Publication Data

Names: Golkar, Golriz, author.
Title: Chloe Kim / by Golriz Golkar.
Description: Minneapolis, MN : Bellwether Media, 2024. | Series: Sports superstars | Includes bibliographical references and index. | Audience: Ages 7-12 | Audience: Grades 4-6 | Summary: "Engaging images accompany information about Chloe Kim. The combination of high-interest subject matter and light text is intended for students in grades 3 through 7"– Provided by publisher.
Identifiers: LCCN 2023006481 (print) | LCCN 2023006482 (ebook) | ISBN 9798886874624 (library binding) | ISBN 9798886876505 (ebook)
Subjects: LCSH: Kim, Chloe, 2000–Juvenile literature. | Snowboarders–United States–Biography–Juvenile literature. | Women Olympic athletes–United States–Biography–Juvenile literature. | Asian American athletes–United States–Biography–Juvenile literature.
Classification: LCC GV857.S57 G68 2024 (print) | LCC GV357.S57 (ebook) | DDC 796.939092 [B]–dc23/eng/20230213
LC record available at https://lccn.loc.gov/2023006481
LC ebook record available at https://lccn.loc.gov/2023006482

Text copyright © 2024 by Bellwether Media, Inc. TORQUE and associated logos are trademarks and/or registered trademarks of Bellwether Media, Inc.

Editor: Rachael Barnes   Designer: Gabriel Hilger

Printed in the United States of America, North Mankato, MN.

TABLE OF CONTENTS

GOING FOR THE GOLD	4
WHO IS CHLOE KIM?	6
A RISING STAR	8
SNOWBOARDING SUPERSTAR	12
A BRIGHT FUTURE	20
GLOSSARY	22
TO LEARN MORE	23
INDEX	24

GOING FOR THE GOLD

It is the 2021 **Winter X Games**. Chloe Kim is getting ready for the **superpipe** event.

She starts her second run. Kim flies up over the snowy pipe. She spins three times. Kim lands a **frontside 1080**! The crowd cheers wildly as she finishes the run. She goes on to win her sixth X Games gold medal!

Two Knocks for Luck

Kim always knocks twice on her snowboard for good luck before every run.

WHO IS CHLOE KIM?

Chloe Kim is a snowboarder. She has won two gold medals at the **Winter Olympics**. She has even set Olympic records! Many people think she is one of the greatest snowboarders of all time.

CHLOE KIM

BIRTHDAY April 23, 2000
HOMETOWN Torrance, California
EVENTS halfpipe and slopestyle
HEIGHT 5 feet 3 inches
JOINED U.S. Ski and Snowboard in 2015

Kim likes to help others. She helped raise money to keep people healthy during the **COVID-19 pandemic**. Kim speaks out against **racism** by sharing her experiences as a proud Korean American.

A RISING STAR

Kim grew up in California with her parents and two sisters. She began snowboarding at age 4. She practiced often in the mountains near her home. By age 6, Kim was snowboarding in junior events. At age 8, she moved to Switzerland to live with her aunt. She trained there for two years.

Kim decided to become a **professional** snowboarder. Olympic snowboarding star Kelly Clark became her **mentor**.

KIM'S FAMILY

8

FAVORITES

HOBBY	FOOD	TV SHOW	OTHER SPORT
			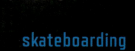
playing guitar	churros	The Office	skateboarding

KIM AND KELLY CLARK IN 2016

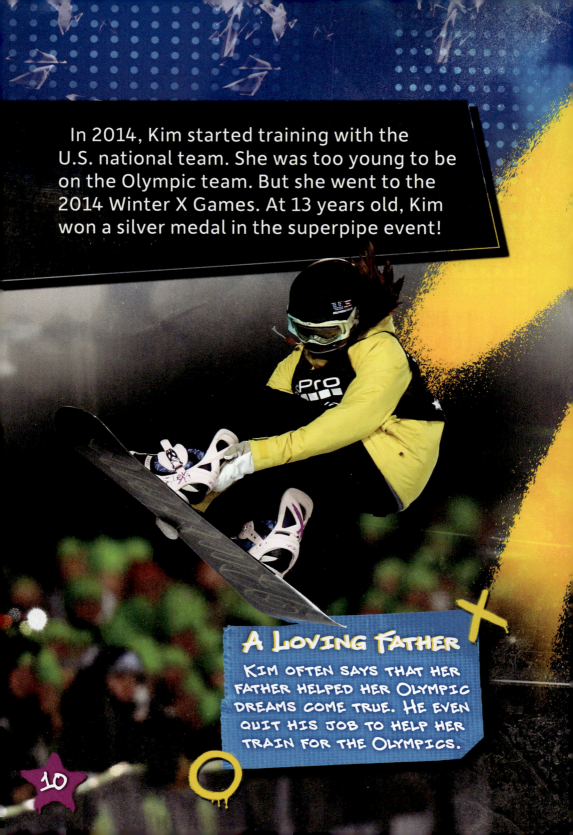

In 2014, Kim started training with the U.S. national team. She was too young to be on the Olympic team. But she went to the 2014 Winter X Games. At 13 years old, Kim won a silver medal in the superpipe event!

A Loving Father

Kim often says that her father helped her Olympic dreams come true. He even quit his job to help her train for the Olympics.

2015 WINTER X GAMES

At the 2015 Winter X Games, Kim won the superpipe gold medal. She became the youngest ever Winter X Games winner.

SNOWBOARDING SUPERSTAR

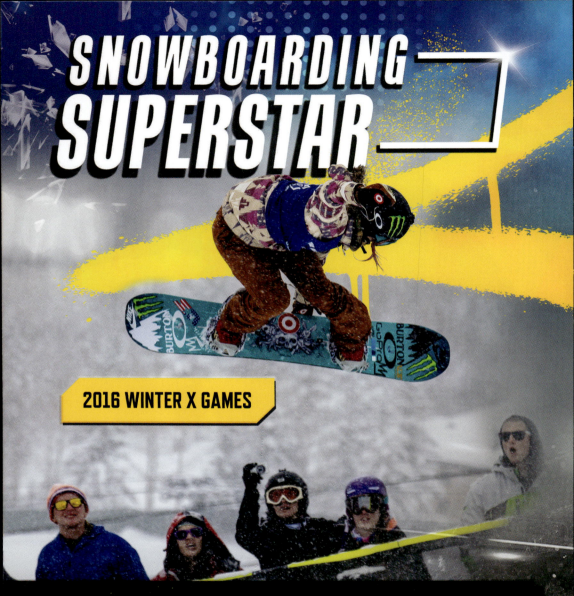

2016 WINTER X GAMES

In 2016, Kim earned her second Winter X Games gold medal. That same year, she took part in the **Winter Youth Olympic Games**. She won gold medals in the **halfpipe** and **slopestyle** events.

She also earned the highest halfpipe score ever in Youth Olympic Games history.

Kim had a record-setting Olympic **debut** in 2018 in Pyeongchang, South Korea. At age 17, she won the gold medal in the women's halfpipe event. Kim became the youngest female Olympic gold medalist in snowboarding history! She also became the first female Olympian to land back-to-back 1080s.

BARBIE GIRL

A look-alike Barbie doll was made of Kim as part of the "Sheroes" collection. The line honored female role models.

2018 WINTER OLYMPICS GOLD MEDAL

Kim won gold again at the 2018 Winter X Games. But she broke her ankle in 2019. She took a break from snowboarding to rest and heal.

Kim studied at Princeton University. When the COVID-19 pandemic began, students were sent home to study. Kim finished her first year of college and returned to snowboarding in 2021.

TIMELINE

— 2014 —
Kim wins her first Winter X Games medal

— 2015 —
Kim wins her first gold medal at the Winter X Games

— 2016 —
Kim wins two gold medals at the Winter Youth Olympic Games

— 2018 —
Kim wins her first Winter Olympics gold medal

— 2022 —
Kim wins her second Winter Olympics gold medal

Kim had her eye on the next Olympic Games. In 2022, she went to the Winter Olympics in Beijing, China. Once again, she took home the gold medal for halfpipe.

She set another record. At age 21, she became the first woman to win two halfpipe gold medals in a row!

2022 WINTER OLYMPICS GOLD MEDAL

TROPHY SHELF

Winter Olympics gold medals
🟢 🟢 snowboarding halfpipe

Winter Youth Olympics gold medals
🔴 halfpipe   🔴 slopestyle

World Championships gold medals
🔵 🔵 snowboarding halfpipe

Winter X Games medals
🔴🔴🔴🔴🔴🔴 gold   🔴 silver   🔴 bronze

19

A BRIGHT FUTURE

After her 2022 Olympic win, Kim took time off from snowboarding. She wanted to rest and try new things. She is looking for acting roles in movies and television.

KIM WITH ACTOR SIMU LIU

Animal Lover

Kim loves animals. She has a dog named Reese. After professional snowboarding, she may work with animals!

Kim plans to snowboard in the 2026 Winter Olympics. She may win another gold medal!

21

GLOSSARY

COVID-19 pandemic—an outbreak of the COVID-19 virus starting in December 2019 that led to shutdowns and millions of deaths around the world

debut—first pro appearance

frontside 1080—a snowboarding trick in which the snowboarder turns their body around three times with their body facing downhill

halfpipe—a U-shaped, high-sided ramp used in snowboarding, skateboarding, and skiing

mentor—a person who gives advice and offers support

professional—related to a player or team that makes money playing a sport

racism—discrimination or hatred based on race

slopestyle—a snowboarding or skiing event in which athletes move down an obstacle course

superpipe—a snow-covered, U-shaped ramp snowboarders and skiers use for their sports; superpipes have walls that are 22 feet (6.7 meters) tall.

Winter Olympics—a worldwide winter sports contest held in a different country every four years

Winter X Games—a yearly extreme sports event that includes snowboarding and skiing

Winter Youth Olympic Games—a worldwide winter sports contest held in a different country every four years for people between the ages of 15 and 18

TO LEARN MORE

AT THE LIBRARY

Chandler, Matt. *Chloe Kim: Gold-Medal Snowboarder*. North Mankato, Minn.: Capstone, 2020.

Gaertner, Meg. *Snowboarding*. Mendota Heights, Minn.: Apex, 2022.

Moon, Derek. *Chloe Kim*. Minneapolis, Minn.: ABDO Publishing, 2019.

ON THE WEB

Factsurfer.com gives you a safe, fun way to find more information.

1. Go to www.factsurfer.com

2. Enter "Chloe Kim" into the search box and click 🔍.

3. Select your book cover to see a list of related content.

23

INDEX

1080, 4, 14
acting, 20
animals, 20
ankle, 16
awards, 4, 6, 10, 11, 12, 13, 14, 15, 16, 18, 19
Barbie, 15
Beijing, China, 18
California, 8
childhood, 8, 10, 11
Clark, Kelly, 8, 9
COVID-19 pandemic, 7, 16
family, 8, 10
favorites, 9
future, 20, 21
halfpipe, 12, 14, 18
knocks, 5

map, 13
Princeton University, 16
profile, 7
Pyeongchang, South Korea, 14
racism, 7
records, 6, 11, 12, 14, 18
slopestyle, 12
superpipe, 4, 10, 11
timeline, 16–17
trophy shelf, 19
U.S. national team, 10
Winter Olympics, 6, 8, 10, 14, 15, 18, 19, 20, 21
Winter X Games, 4, 10, 11, 12, 16
Winter Youth Olympic Games, 12, 13

The images in this book are reproduced through the courtesy of: REUTERS/ Alamy, front cover; Tim Clayton - Corbis/ Contributor/ Getty Images, pp. 3, 7; Kelsey Brunner/ The Aspen Times/ AP Images, pp. 4, 4-5; Angelika Warmuth/ picture-alliance/ dpa/ AP Images, pp. 6-7; sharpener, p. 7 (American flag); Joe Scarnici/ Stringer/ Getty Images, p. 8; Tom Pennington/ Staff/ Getty Images, p. 9; RemarkEliza, p. 9 (playing guitar); AGCuesta, p. 9 (churros); Rokas Tenys/ Alamy, p. 9 (*The Office*); nito, p. 9 (skateboarding); Doug Pensinger/ Staff/ Getty Images, p. 10; Daniel Petty/ Contributor/ Getty Images, p. 11; Liz Copan/ AP Images, p. 12; IOC/ Handout/ Getty Images, pp. 13, 16; Action Plus Sports Images/ Alamy, p. 13 (Oslo); Leonard Zhukovsky, p. 13 (Pyeongchang), 17 (gold medal); Cavan Images/ Alamy, p. 13 (Aspen); calvin86, p. 13 (Beijing); Gregory Bull/ AP Images, pp. 14, 20-21; Morry Gash/ AP Images, p. 15; Ezra Shaw/ Staff/ Getty Images, pp. 16-17; Hendrik Schmidt/ picture-alliance/ dpa/ AP Images, p. 17 (2022); Tim Clayton - Corbis/ Contributor/ Getty Images, pp. 18-19; Frank Augstein/ AP Images, p. 19; Mary DeCicco/ Stringer/ Getty Images, p. 20; Ramsey Cardy/ Contributor/ Getty Images, p. 23.

24